SUPER SCIENCE FEATS:
MEDICAL BREAKTHROUGHS
VACCINES

by Alicia Z. Klepeis

Ideas for Parents and Teachers

Pogo Books let children practice reading informational text while introducing them to nonfiction features such as headings, labels, sidebars, maps, and diagrams, as well as a table of contents, glossary, and index.

Carefully leveled text with a strong photo match offers early fluent readers the support they need to succeed.

Before Reading

- "Walk" through the book and point out the various nonfiction features. Ask the student what purpose each feature serves.
- Look at the glossary together. Read and discuss the words.

Read the Book

- Have the child read the book independently.
- Invite him or her to list questions that arise from reading.

After Reading

- Discuss the child's questions. Talk about how he or she might find answers to those questions.
- Prompt the child to think more. Ask: How do vaccines help keep us healthy? Can you think of any other ways to stay healthy?

Pogo Books are published by Jump!
5357 Penn Avenue South
Minneapolis, MN 55419
www.jumplibrary.com

Copyright © 2021 Jump!
International copyright reserved in all countries.
No part of this book may be reproduced in any form without written permission from the publisher.

Library of Congress Cataloging-in-Publication Data

Names: Klepeis, Alicia, 1971- author.
Title: Vaccines / by Alicia Z. Klepeis.
Description: Minneapolis, MN: Jump!, Inc., [2021]
Series: Super science feats: medical breakthroughs
Includes index. | Audience: Ages 7-10
Identifiers: LCCN 2020029989 (print)
LCCN 2020029990 (ebook)
ISBN 9781645278016 (hardcover)
ISBN 9781645278023 (paperback)
ISBN 9781645278030 (ebook)
Subjects: LCSH: Vaccines—Juvenile literature.
Vaccination—Juvenile literature.
Classification: LCC RA638 .K64 2021 (print)
LCC RA638 (ebook) | DDC 615.3/72—dc23
LC record available at https://lccn.loc.gov/2020029989
LC ebook record available at https://lccn.loc.gov/2020029990

Editor: Eliza Leahy
Designer: Michelle Sonnek

Photo Credits: mangostock/Shutterstock, cover; Sergiy Kuzmin/Shutterstock, 1; Bomshtein/Shutterstock, 3; New Africa/Shutterstock, 4, 19; Dragon Images/Shutterstock, 5; sharpner/Shutterstock, 6-7 (background); Wellcome Images/Science Source, 6-7 (drawings); DEA PICTURE LIBRARY/Getty, 8-9; Science History Images/Alamy, 10-11; studiovin/Shutterstock, 12; Zinkevych/iStock, 13; Arturs Budkevics/Shutterstock, 14-15; kendo_OK/Shutterstock, 16-17 (background); Science Photo Library/Alamy, 16-17 (screen); AnthiaCumming/iStock, 18; AshTproductions/Shutterstock, 20-21; catshila/Shutterstock, 23.

Printed in the United States of America at Corporate Graphics in North Mankato, Minnesota.

TABLE OF CONTENTS

CHAPTER 1

. . . .

STOPPING THE SPREAD

Have you had the flu shot? It is a **vaccine**. It is just one of many. They keep us healthy. How? They keep us from getting sick.

Forms of them were used thousands of years ago. People in ancient India and China used them to fight **diseases**. They still work to fight diseases today.

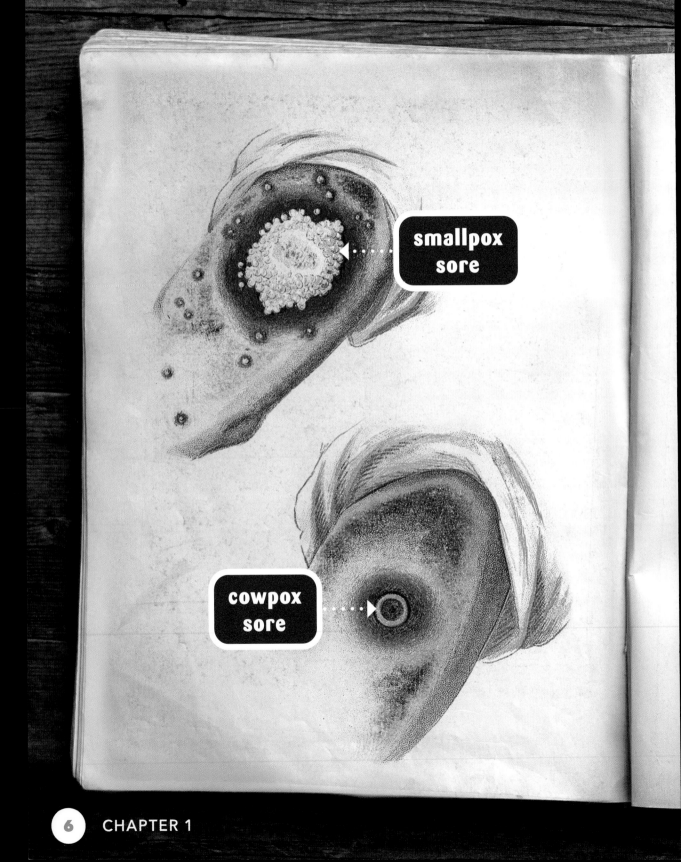

Vaccines as we know them have been around since the 1700s. In 1768, many people in England were sick. Some had cowpox. Others had smallpox. Both cause rashes and fever.

Dr. John Fewster discovered something. Some people could fight off smallpox. How? They had been **exposed** to cowpox first.

DID YOU KNOW?

The last known case of smallpox was in 1977. Cowpox is rare today.

Dr. Edward Jenner studied this further in 1796. He took **pus** from a cowpox sore. He put it in a cut on a boy's arm. What happened? The boy got cowpox.

Then Jenner took pus from a smallpox sore. He put it in the same boy's arm. Did the boy get sick? No! What did this show? The cowpox had acted as a vaccine. This was big news!

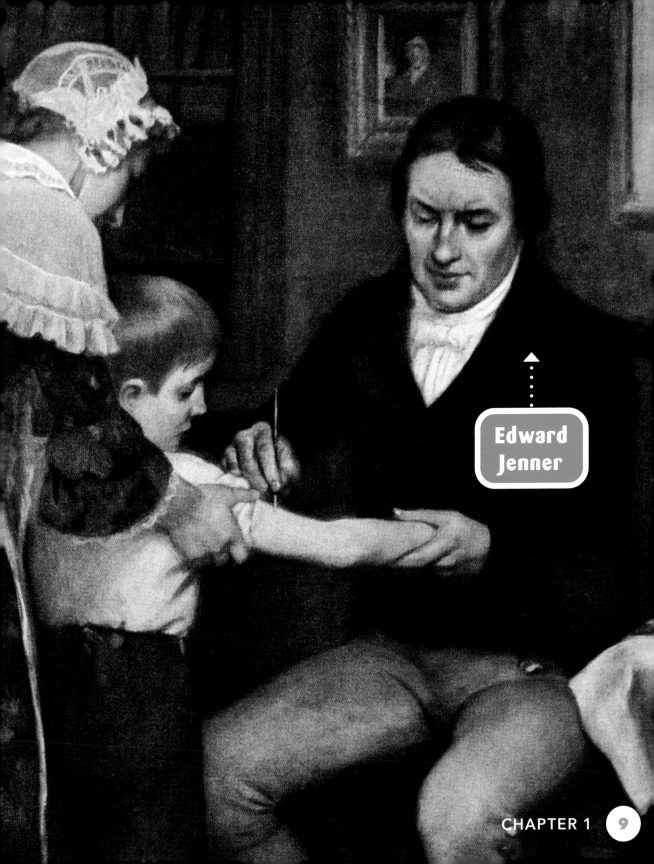

Edward Jenner

Scientist Louis Pasteur built on Jenner's work. How? He made more vaccines. One was for rabies. This often spreads by animal bites.

DID YOU KNOW?

Pets get shots, too. Like what? Dogs and cats get rabies shots. Dogs can get a flu shot, too. It is different from the one we get!

CHAPTER 2

· ·

HOW THEY WORK

Vaccines were a medical **breakthrough**. They stop the spread of disease. How do they work? Let's learn!

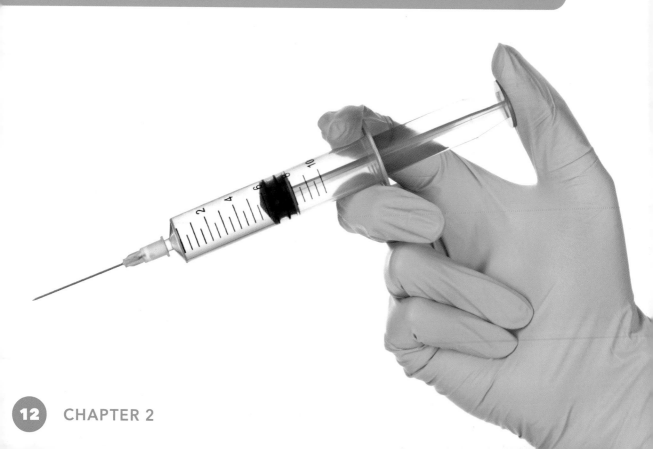

Let's say your friend gets the flu. You don't get sick. Why? You had your flu shot.

Shots have **germs** in them. Some have dead germs. Others have weak germs. Some have tiny germ pieces. They enter your body. How? Some are in a **syringe**. The needle pokes you. Others come in a nose spray.

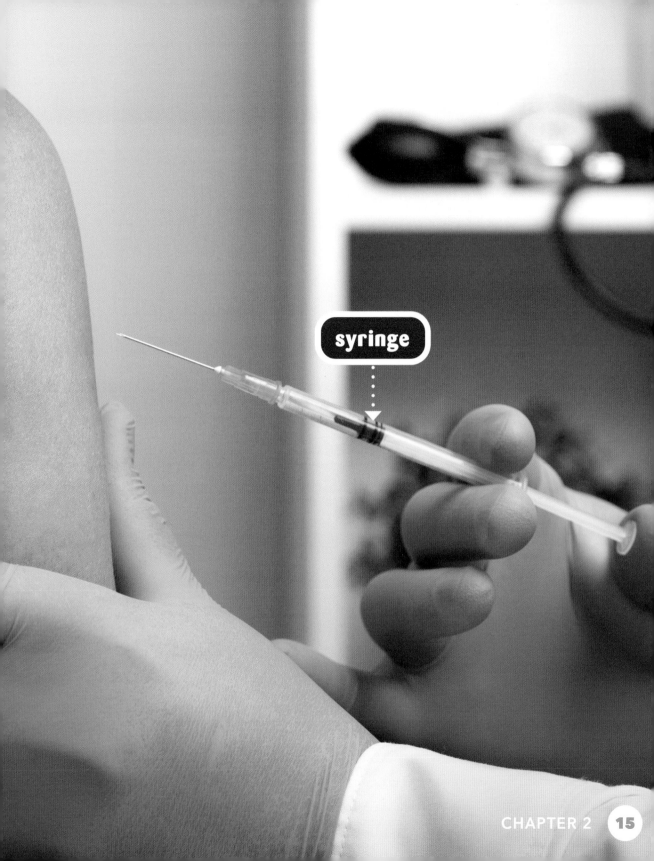

syringe

Germs have **antigens**. They alert your **immune system**. What happens? It makes **antibodies**. These attach to antigens. They tell the immune system to destroy the germs. The antibodies stay in your body. What if the disease enters your body later? The antibodies remember. They fight it off.

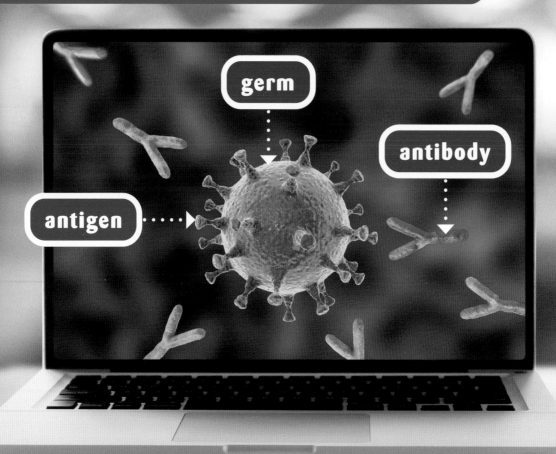

germ

antibody

antigen

TAKE A LOOK!

You get a shot. What happens? Take a look!

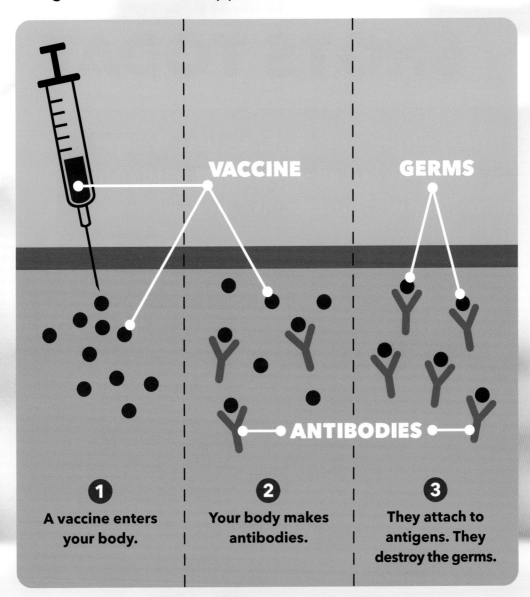

VACCINE

GERMS

ANTIBODIES

1 A vaccine enters your body.

2 Your body makes antibodies.

3 They attach to antigens. They destroy the germs.

CHAPTER 3

GETTING SHOTS TODAY

Many people get shots today. We get flu shots. What else? We get shots for measles and mumps. We get them for chicken pox, too.

Some people cannot get shots. Why? They might have weak immune systems. Shots can make them sick. But other people can help keep them safe. How? They can get shots. This makes it harder for diseases to spread.

Vaccines are important. In 2020, COVID-19 spread across the world. At first, there was no vaccine for it. Scientists quickly went to work. By the end of the year, there were several COVID-19 vaccines.

Vaccines stop the spread of disease. They save millions of lives each year!

DID YOU KNOW?

There was a flu **pandemic** in 1918. Many people got sick. About 50 million died. Now we have the flu shot. It saves thousands of lives each year.

ACTIVITIES & TOOLS

TRY THIS!

MAKE YOUR OWN SANITIZER

Vaccines help protect against diseases. Handwashing does, too. If you don't have access to soap, you can use hand sanitizer. You can make your own! Be sure to have an adult help. If you have a pair of plastic gloves handy, wear them when preparing this mixture.

What You Need:

- 2/3 cup of 91 percent rubbing alcohol
- 1/3 cup of aloe vera gel
- a few drops of tea tree or peppermint oil (optional)
- small bowl
- whisk
- funnel
- 4 to 6 2-ounce squeeze bottles

❶ Wash your hands and kitchen gear thoroughly before starting.

❷ Place the rubbing alcohol, aloe vera gel, and oil (if using) into a small bowl.

❸ Use a whisk to stir until they are mixed thoroughly.

❹ Use a funnel to pour the mixture into the squeeze bottles. Leave a little room at the top of each bottle. That way, you can shake it before using to be sure it is mixed well.

GLOSSARY

antibodies: Proteins produced by the immune system in response to foreign substances like viruses.

antigens: Substances that cause the body to form antibodies.

breakthrough: An important discovery or advance in knowledge.

diseases: Sicknesses, especially those with specific symptoms or which affect a specific part of the body.

exposed: Subjected to risk from a harmful condition.

germs: Microscopic living things, especially those which cause disease.

immune system: The system of the body that protects us from disease or illness.

pandemic: A worldwide outbreak of a disease.

pus: A cloudy, often yellowish fluid formed at a place of infection.

syringe: A device used to inject fluids into or withdraw fluids from the body.

vaccine: A substance usually given by injection to people or animals to protect against disease.

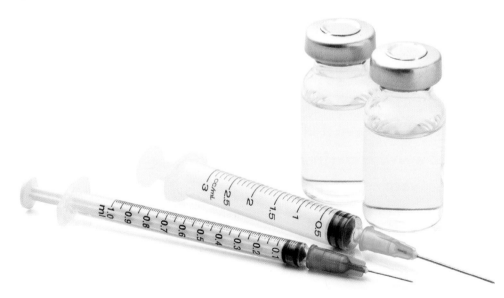

INDEX

TO LEARN MORE

Finding more information is as easy as 1, 2, 3.

❶ **Go to www.factsurfer.com**

❷ **Enter "vaccines" into the search box.**

❸ **Choose your book to see a list of websites.**

FACT SURFER